In Transit

In Transit

POEMS

Nicholas Pierce

WINNER OF THE NEW CRITERION POETRY PRIZE

Criterion Books
NEW YORK

First American edition published in 2021 by Criterion Books, an imprint of Encounter Books, an activity of Encounter for Culture and Education, Inc., a nonprofit, tax-exempt corporation.
www.newcriterion.com/poetryprize

Library of Congress Cataloging-in-Publication Data

Names: Pierce, Nicholas, 1990– author.
Title: In Transit: Poems / Nicholas Pierce.
Description: First American edition. | New York : Criterion Books, 2021. |
Identifiers: LCCN 2021033826 | ISBN 9781641772471 (hardcover)
Subjects: LCGFT: Poetry.
LCC PS3616.I35646 I5 2021 | DDC 811/.6–dc23
LC record available at https://lccn.loc.gov/2021033826

Contents

III

Acknowledgments

Grateful acknowledgment is made to the editors of the following journals, in which some of these poems originally appeared: *32 Poems*, *The Adroit Journal*, *Alabama Literary Review*, *Birmingham Poetry Review*, *The Hopkins Review*, *Measure Review*, and *Subtropics*.

For help editing and arranging the poems in this book, my deepest gratitude to John Poch, Erin O'Luanaigh, Allie Field Bell, Joe Arredondo, Forester McClatchey, Diana Clarke, and Ryan Pierce. Thanks also to my classmates at the University of Utah and at the University of Florida, as well as to my professors Jackie Osherow, Katharine Coles, Ange Mlinko, William Logan, and Michael Hofmann.

for my mother

In Transit

New Weather

Dust settling on the windshield,
on blacktop, on mesquite and yucca.

Dust atomizing the grazing cattle.
Eroding distance. Subtracting all color

save red from West Texas. Dust
venting into the car, a particle haze,

the lingering cloud of a compact
snapped shut and stowed away

in the secret depths of a mother's purse.
Breathed in, sneezed out. Terrifying

to her two boys in the backseat,
whose Southern California childhood

never acquainted them with weather.
Merely irritating to her husband,

who thinks it best to keep driving
despite the litany of taillights

glaring from the roadside. Vanishing.
Who capitulates, begrudgingly,

when raindrops black as crude oil
begin to sludge the windshield,

mascara tears that leave behind
blinding trails as they trickle down,

reducing the world to a car's interior.
To darkness. Sound. The crunch of gravel

when they reach, they hope, the shoulder.
The sibilance of tires tearing past.

The mother bracing for impact
while telling her boys not to worry.

An eternity of waiting. And then
a splitting light—rain washing away

the mud caul, restoring the desert,
their eyes opening as if for the first time.

I

Agave

The agave blooms once and only once
in its ten-plus year lifespan,
unsheathing a penile projection

that grows as high as twenty-five feet
and terminates in an alien bouquet
of yellow flowers, as if in memory

of itself; for the stalk's emergence
sets in motion a ticking clock,
the revolution of its long shadow

keeping time till the end. Even then
the agave looks every bit as hostile
as the places it prefers to live.

A sea urchin of the high desert,
a grenade frozen mid-explosion,
it retains the same lurid shape

of rosette from birth to senescence,
with leaves that taper to needlepoints,
ensuring no one gets too close.

But this tough face belies a soft heart
flush with the jimador's prized tequila,
as the grape is flush with wine, the student

with potential. Joe gave me one once,
in a pot the blue of deep water,
which I stationed in a corner of my desk,

next to the vintage typewriter,
the record player collecting dust,
below my window but beyond the purview

of sunlight, where I wish I could say
I forgot about the plant. In truth
I simply neglected to water it

for weeks, then months, as its leaves
freckled like banana peels, retreating
from my touch in slow motion,

falling off. When I returned the gift,
my mentor saved it the only way
he knew how, by planting it in his garden.

The Invisible World

I.

A young Kerouac eyes the nude
who shares his perch on the top shelf
of Joe's bookcase. Both photographs
celebrate male beauty, the self,

though one is a reproduction.
Another Beat, two shelves below,
fills the gap between Bukowski
and Carver. Oddly apropos,

a port bottle props up the books.
Religion has its own section;
poetry too. *The Other Bible*
looms over posthumous Sexton,

whose *Awful Rowing Toward God*
lists to starboard — or rather, Starbuck.
Joe's former protégés, students
like myself ("a strapping young buck"),

compose the heart of the bookcase.
Their portraits range in size, perhaps
in accordance with importance.
Six (I keep count) minutes elapse

after Joe calls out, "Almost ready!"
We're headed to the museum
to see a new retrospective
on Magritte, who amuses him.

* * *

Then Joe offers his perspective:
"Notice how—it's quite discreet—
light comes from the left foreground
rather than outside. Magritte

sought to replicate a stage."
He traces with his pinky nail,
which extends a full inch beyond
his fingertip, a key detail—

the shadow shaped like a sickle
obscuring half the rock's right side.
"Here we see in miniature
how the painter, petrified

though he was of such readings,
veils the very world he depicts—
yes, as with the rock. He is
both the light source and eclipse."

2.

Unlike the eye, the mind's eye apprehends
few differences between us: thrice my age,
Joe rarely acts it, even at this stage
of the night, when our conversation tends
to lose steam, and he—having cooked—pretends
not to mind cleaning up. Often, I'll page
through his *New Yorkers*, see what's all the rage
in poetry these days, or text old friends—

but not tonight. Tonight, I sit and think,
swirling my wine, watching the dregs go round,
a blizzard blotting out the lamplight drowned
in my half-empty glass, while at the sink
Joe scrubs our plates, using his pinky nail
to scratch off remnants peeking out like Braille.

Erōmenos

One night, while eating dinner on Joe's roof,
    wine-drunk and self-important, we conducted
    our very own symposium on love,
with each guest venturing a definition.
    First up was John: a Christian, husband, dad,
    he thought that earthly love approximated
what lay in store for us in the next life.
    James, smart but saddled with a surfer's accent,
    believed that love was just a word we used
so that attraction wouldn't seem so vulgar.
    Johnnie—whose photographs revealed, to all,
    it seemed, but his best friend and muse, J. Eric,
the feelings he had for and kept from him—
    considered love impossible to capture
    in words because it was at odds with thought.
J. Eric, who had grown up farming cotton,
    sought to define love through analogy,
    claiming that it was like the plant's raw fibers,
which, once refined, would clothe and keep us warm.
    Before I took my turn, Joe interrupted
    to serve dessert: grilled peaches from his tree,
topped with whipped cream and a balsamic drizzle.
    While we dug in, he roasted coffee beans
    in an air popper, waiting for the second—
always the second—crack to pour the beans
    into the mouth of a hand mill, an antique,
    then cranking, cranking, cranking, switching arms,
then cranking some more, till the wooden drawer
    was close to overflowing with that fine

brown powder; then he went downstairs, returning
with six of his most beautiful clay cups.
  Mine, as with all the others, was imperfect,
    having been made by hand—by student hands,
most likely, since the artists Joe collected
    were largely students who had once, like us,
    attended dinners on his roof, discussing
the subjects we discussed, eating the food
    we ate; who, as we would, had graduated
    and moved away, keeping in touch or not.
"Love," I began, uncertain how to go on,
    looking around the table, at the plates
    stacked up, the faces waiting for an answer;
at Joe, our Socrates, my closest friend,
    who lived alone in an Art Deco rental
    with paint chips flaking off the outside walls
and water stains collecting on the ceiling,
    and who expected nothing in return
    for all he gave us, which was more than plenty—
more, anyway, than I could often eat.
    That's love, I thought, while at the same time thinking
    of Joe's foot running up and down my leg,
a gesture that I told myself meant nothing,
    which I (admit it) even sort of liked,
    since no one else received such special treatment.
"Love is attention by another name,"
    I said at last, and left it at that, waiting,
    despite myself, for Joe's approving touch.

North of the Border

A hand pushing on my shoulder
rouses me. "Listen," Joe says,
and his tone conveys
why, the air instantly colder
as the crackle of gunfire
starts again and then stops.
As we wait for Border Patrol or the cops
to shed light on our dire
situation, and for the hundred or so
other campers at El Cosmico

to react, we run through our choices,
running among them; though
with nowhere to go
but our car and the noises—
fainter now—coming from the direction
of the parking lot, we decide
it best to stay put, to hide
in our tent until protection
arrives, whatever and whenever
that may be, if ever.

"Could they be closer than we think,"
Joe asks, "or further away?"
I wonder who he pictures "they"
to be, if that ink-
blot of a word conjures the same
murky images for us both,
of drug traffickers in a deal gone south

taking stock and then aim;
or if he sees instead
(the thought passed through my head)

gunmen going tent to tent.
I wonder, too, if this is how
it feels to be an embryo,
as I cocoon myself—ignorant
and terrified of every sound—
in my sleeping bag
and pray that the night won't drag
on much longer, until finally, around
dawn, I fall back to sleep,
only to be awakened by the beep

of Joe's phone minutes later,
reminding me that our tour
through Chinati begins in an hour.
We unzip our incubator
and scramble out, in our rush
forgetting all about the nightmare
that was our night. Like a nightmare,
it comes back in flashes, a hush
descending over the car
after I bring up the bizarre

experience, less than relieved
when Joe confirms that it occurred—
or that he at least heard
what at the time he believed
to be a shootout, stressing "at the time."

I lean my head against my window
and count the fenceposts
into town, struggling to rhyme
how we felt mere hours ago
with how we feel now.

Yesterday, we listened to a docent
go on about Judd's "mastery
over the plastic arts," leaving no mystery
unsolved in his (admittedly cogent)
interpretations. We expect
that today's tour will go similarly,
but—perhaps because it's so early—
our guide keeps his intellect
mostly to himself, instructing us
only not to touch. Thus,

as we make our way through
the first artillery shed—
a long brick building that Judd
converted into a gallery—we forget (or I do) ·
that we're not alone with the boxes
and speak candidly
about valuing each other's company,
which must seem obnoxious
to our observer, who must feel,
whatever our feelings, like a third wheel.

The boxes are arranged in three
evenly spaced rows. Made
from mill aluminum — the highest grade —
and polished to near-transparency,
they transform as sunlight
strikes them from different angles,
at one instant glimmering like spangles
and at another appearing white
and depthless, as a lake will
when the sun is at its zenith. The mill

aluminum is so sensitive to oils
that it can carry a fingerprint
for years, as is painfully evident
when I kneel down and one all but spoils
my reflection. Then comes a *POP!*
POP! POP!, our guide stepping in
to explain that this can happen when
the warming metal expands. We get up
from the floor, laughing off our mistake,
though the fear is harder to shake.

A Night at The Lightning Field

Up late reading *Cloud Atlas*,
José asleep in the bed next to mine,
I press my ear against the cabin wall,
thinking I've heard my name.

On the other side are three women,
classmates in our field course,
friends. They're talking about Joe,
who joined us in Marfa last weekend,

driving down from Lubbock
with a cooler full of pancake batter
and Topo Chico. I can make out
only so much through their laughter,

but my sense is that they're joking
about how Joe put his hand on my back
at breakfast. I don't blame them
for wondering why a college student

would be friends with a man
in his sixties, for imagining what we do
behind closed doors—but it hurts
just the same. Returning to my novel,

I'm surprised to find myself tearing up
over Frobisher's letters to Sixsmith,
their romance devoid of troublesome
particulars, wistful, chaste, gay.

José sleeps heavily, no doubt exhausted
from being stuck behind the wheel
for hours, only to get us here
after dark. Intent on seeing sunrise

reflected in the poles, he set his alarm
for 5:00 a.m., I recall with a sigh
as I lay my head on the pillow,
still reeling from Frobisher's suicide.

In the morning, the poles fade
as if into existence, changing from black
to blue to blue streaked with pink,
at odds and at one with all they mirror—

the clay field pocked with hoofmarks,
the windmill threatening to begin
its daily rotation, the mountains
holding back the light as long as they can,

and the light, too. The poles ignite
like struck matches, one by one,
then row by row, till the whole grid
is aflame. I can't be sure if what I heard

is what they said; can't tell who is who
as my friends wander through the field,
silhouettes in a stainless steel forest,
shadows whose features I fill in.

II

After My Mother's Wedding

On her rusted-out patio chairs, we drank
late into the evening, my brother and I; drank
a cheap California red with a twist top
and talked about a woman we had seen
outside the café that morning, a brunette
in a bright yellow pea coat and bright
red shoes—bright as a handful of wildflowers
along a highway. We could not believe
how beautiful she was, this woman,
on that bike of hers. The motion of her knees
rolling below the hem of her dress
looked something like driftwood in a wave,
I thought, wistfully, before taking another swig
and leaning back in my chair, brushing
the young orange tree (a wedding gift
from my brother) in a terracotta pot
beside the table. Its trembling branches
were like the fingers of an outstretched hand,
I thought, again wistfully, as I staggered
out of my seat, through the yard and,
under a sky empty of stars, onto the old
trampoline, sinking into its weatherworn skin
so that I could see the neighboring houses.

Katabasis for E.

Just hear me out. I'm going to describe
a night of little consequence in terms
of what occurred, and yet on which I've dwelled
for going on three years. "Dwelled" isn't right;
more accurately (but still incorrect),
I've merely not forgotten it, unlike
so many of our nights together, which
have coalesced because of their resemblance
to one another, forming in my mind
a single night that finds us gossiping
about our cohort and in the same breath
complaining that our lives, as MFAS,
play out on stage, all the while downing wine
till we collapse on her misshapen loveseat
to watch another screwball comedy.

The night in question started out the same,
but ended with us stripping by the pool—
stripping, but only to our underwear.
(Before I go much further, I should say
that at the time we'd yet to even kiss;
had, like the couples in those black-and-white
Hollywood movies, made flirtatious banter
into an art, getting around the code
of friendship with suggestive glances and
emoji-ridden texts. To tell the truth,
it was my fault that we remained just friends;
for loving her, I thought, meant giving up
on poetry. Faust's bargain, Yeats's choice—

before that evening I took these for facts,
not, as they were, excuses to account
for the missed chances that make up a life.)

So there we were, half-naked by the pool—
half-naked, though she'd skinny-dipped with friends
the night before, or so she'd claimed upstairs,
bringing it up in such an offhand way
(as though it were her normal, every-night
behavior), that I'd dared her on the spot
to go with me. No, not to prove her wrong;
I did it to confirm that my impression
of her, which couldn't have been more removed
from how her stories made her come across,
was right. I simply couldn't picture her
stripping before an audience, not least
an audience of writers known to flaunt
their most egregious moments in their work,
and so was unsurprised but disappointed
when she stopped short of doing so with me.

We'd been discussing, and continued to
while testing the black water with our toes,
what separates good writers from great ones.
In her opinion, it came down to luck,
not passion, time, or effort, as I thought
(or wanted to believe), but plain dumb luck:
"The dirty secret of all writing programs
is that while fundamentals can be taught,
true talent can't be." She herself could *feel*
her way through lines as musical as those

I spent days coming up with (if not longer),
and since hers were the product not of thought
but that which animates the hand before
the mind's involvement—call it intuition—
they sounded less contrived, more true to life.
But were they really? Why should truth come easy?

We were surrounded on all sides but one
by the imposing towers of her complex.
I'd been there probably a hundred times;
a hundred times had paced behind the gate
until I heard her footsteps coming down
the stairs, waiting there to receive the key
that would admit me, that she'd always toss
from the same landing, always the third floor's,
and that I'd almost always catch before
climbing to her—two stairs at a time, always.
But never once, among those hundred visits,
had I considered why she tossed, instead
of walked, the key to me . . . Was it a test?
I asked myself this question as I watched
her dive in and, because the pool reflected
a star-strewn sky, appear to rise while falling.

My eyes then drifted to the lighted windows
that gave onto apartments just like hers:
the same cheap furniture, the same white walls,
only without the prints of Frank Sinatra
and Judy Garland, not to mention all
her other icons (Mary, Christ, the saints)—
without, that is, the things that made her *her*.

But who was that? And who was I to say?
I was still standing there when she got out,
so lost in thought that seconds, maybe a
whole minute, passed before I noticed how
her soaked-through clothing clung to her wet body,
revealing two faint areolas and
the curve of her breasts—which, as she inhaled,
rose and fell, rose and fell. In retrospect,
I'm certain that this was the moment when

I fell for her. And though I'm also certain
that she expected me to kiss her then,
my only proof is that her eyes were closed—
just as they were when, on the night we met,
after a few too many drinks at dinner,
we lingered on a sidewalk near my house,
at one point lying down, our elbows touching.
I still remember what went through my head—
the second-guessing that at last succeeded
in keeping me from taking, so to speak,
the plunge—because those very thoughts resurfaced
as the pool water chilled my feet, which I'd
placed ever so discreetly next to hers,
and I considered what would happen if
I stopped resisting; stopped not leaning in.
Then the time came to act. It came and went.

What's left to tell? She dried off, went upstairs,
and two nights later, we resumed our old
routine of drinking wine and gossiping
and watching Cary Grant win back his wife,

only now, when the credits rolled to black,
I was a little slower to stand up—
and slower still the next night, and the next,
until at length we found ourselves in love,
then out of love, then in it once again,
ad infinitum. And I'd often wonder,
through these vicissitudes, if we *had* kissed
that night, would we have ended up together?
The truth is, it's impossible to know;
but nights when I remember how it felt
to hear her footsteps coming down the stairs,
her jingling keys, I can't help thinking so.

How Do You Wear Your Nakedness?

1.

The performance begins for real
when we re-enter Uferstudios,
having been sent out and called back in
by the two dancers who now pose

in matching white button-downs,
army boots, and—as revealed by the fan
breathing life into the scene—
nothing else. For an American

unaccustomed to nudity on TV,
much less in person, outside a bedroom,
I surprise myself by keeping calm
when the female dancer—in whom

I see a young Charlotte Gainsbourg—
starts to work up a sweat on stage,
stretching, jumping rope, cartwheeling,
in the process succeeding to engage

as well as embarrass the audience.
Of course, we're supposed to laugh
at the absurdity of her routine,
and it *is* funny how her top half

seems oblivious to the peep show
downstairs; but the energy she exerts
to achieve this laugh—at one point
running in place until it hurts

just to watch—has me wondering
if we're not also meant to feel
a little guilty for being here,
for taking pleasure in her dishabille.

Moreover, it has me questioning
the paces I put myself through
to package an experience in, say,
rhyming quatrains, making much ado

about, if not nothing, not much.
And for what? To cover up the fact
that minus rhyme and quatrain
said experience would attract

scant interest? A sad thought, that,
and one that fails to factor in
the propelling role each plays
in the writing process—a role akin

to that of the orchestral music
adding a welcome note of irony
(and perhaps also of sophistication)
to the proceedings, which now see

the dancers performing a waltz
while clutching each other by
not the waist or back but the crotch.
At this point, no one bats an eye

at the oddity of two strangers
fondling each other as they weave
between bouquets of white lilies
sprouting out of what I believe

are the kind of plastic water jugs
found in break rooms everywhere,
and which amount to the only props
on an otherwise empty—no, *bare*—

stage. What is shocking, though,
is how quickly, once shirts and boots
come off, we all adjust to the sight
of the dancers in their birthday suits,

even tire of it—which is the point,
I think, since as it runs its course,
their act more and more recalls
a marriage heading toward divorce.

2.

"How do you wear your nakedness?"
asks the man to my right, who crosses
and re-crosses his legs as he waits
for an answer. "It's a long process,"

the male dancer at last responds,
"getting to where you're at ease
with the idea of disclosing yourself,
fully, on stage; to where your knees

don't shake at the mere thought of it.
But eventually, at least in my case,
you come to find it freeing—not how
a mask is freeing, for your face

couldn't be more visible. No,
it's closer to how you feel following
a confession, as though a burden
had been lifted. The strange thing—

the thing I couldn't have predicted—
is that audiences tend to find
our being naked more embarrassing
than we do, though I'm inclined

to think that if they sat through
our act as many times as we have,
they wouldn't greet the appearance
of our genitals with such grave

expressions. What do you think,
Lily?" His partner gives him a look
that asks "Do I have to answer?"
then, sighing, closes the notebook

in which she's been keeping track
of everything we've had to say
or else doodling to pass the time
during this post-performance Q&A.

"Well," she begins, "I don't mean
to sound dismissive, but I disagree
with the premise of the question,
which assumes that we wear nudity

in the same way we wear clothing,
when in truth—and you'd know this
if you ever stripped in public—
nudity is the absence of artifice,

of adornment. When you're naked,
you have nothing to hide behind,
nothing to mask how exposed you feel,
and so must learn to pay no mind

to the feeling, to any feeling, really;
must trust that your body knows
what to do, that it will continue
to move even when the routine goes

in directions you didn't anticipate,
wouldn't *want* to anticipate, since
opening yourself up to surprise
is the only way to keep the audience

on its toes." In the ensuing silence,
I find myself staring at the bouquets
of white lilies, trying to picture
how they'd look in different displays,

wondering if the blue water jugs
bring out their beauty or diminish it,
being themselves rather plain,
if not downright ugly; and I admit

that by the end of the Q&A,
I'm no closer to a point of view,
seeing both sides for what they are:
incompatible and yet nakedly true.

Wonderwall

A busker in a donkey mask serenades Charlie
with a soulless cover of "Wonderwall."
The wall at his back, once snaking past Checkpoint Charlie,
finds new life as a gallery that Charlie
decides not to see to the end, for to the west
waits the Mauerpark market, and she—Charlie,
that is ("My name is Charlotte, but friends call me Charlie")—
hears that the treasures are scooped up before
noon, and it's a quarter till. We're halfway there before
I consider how strange it is that Charlie
invited me along, using Google Translate
no less, hardly the most reliable translator;

that a girl so—in a phrase I have to translate
despite its self-evidence—out of my league as Charlie
would want my company. Is she translating
my willingness as mere kindness, while I translate
her kindness as innocence, or using me as a wall
to keep away the men who would translate
an unaccompanied woman as one in need (translation:
as a target)? As the S-Bahn crosses into West
Berlin, our conversation migrates to West
Texas, "where even native speakers need a translator,
the accents are so . . ." My joke falls flat before
her phone can spell it out in German, and before

I know it, the two of us are standing before
a book vendor, she doing her best to translate,
and I, like the Ethan Hawke character in *Before
Sunrise*, acting as if I understand. Before
today—aside from when I stumbled on Checkpoint Charlie,
pausing to watch couples snap selfies before
the immortalized shack and to glance at before-
and-after-reunification photos of the Wall—
I managed to avoid tourist traps like the Wall
section preserved for East Side Gallery. Before
I met Charlie, little appealed to me west
of Museum Island, itself crowded with westerners.

Now, everywhere I look—north, south, east, west—
are the sort of tourists who, placed before
a map of Germany in '89, wouldn't know west
from the GDR. Growing up in southwestern
Germany, in an area I'd know from translations
of the Brothers Grimm, were they not so westernized,
gave my companion a fairytale sense of the West
as somewhere to escape to. When I ask if Charlie
is ready to flee the market (painful as Charley
horses, my puns), in reality I mean West
Berlin. I mean, too, to give her an out: if at the Wall
all she sought was a friend, I've been the wall

preventing her from finding one. I have Walser
in my backpack; what more do I need? "In the West
they call this 'cowardice,' this building of walls
for fear of getting hurt," I nearly say, sensing the wall
going up between us, seeing through it. Before
I can, though, she leads me to Berlin's glorified Walmart,
Kaufhaus des Westerns, to show me a "wall
of fish." An exaggeration or mistranslation,
either way packed with salmon soon to be translated
into fillets, into nutrients and shit, her "wall"
sweats in a corner of the food court. Charlie
exhales and on the fogged glass writes "Charlie

& Nick." I note the ampersand, hurt that Charlie
didn't use a heart. Two salmon hug the wall
as if to read her message. Wide-eyed and westward-
bound (though forced to change direction before
too long), they mouth a prayer we don't have to translate.

The Shirt of Nessus

Forcing a thumb inside, juice
hemorrhaging from the entry wound,
S. deposits bits of dimpled peel

in her lounge chair's cupholder,
then halves and halves again
the jaundiced globe, a cataclysm

writ small. Citrus suffuses the air,
overwhelming the smell of seawater
drying on her skin, the Aegean

put briefly out of mind, reduced
to a metronomic crashing,
mere turquoise on the periphery.

We were a long time getting here
and would have been longer
had those two women not driven by,

pulling onto the narrow margin
of the jackknifing mountain road
we'd found ourselves back on,

after a brief detour down a dirt path
led us not to the beach, as we'd hoped,
but to the doorstep of a family

setting the table for Sunday brunch.
They sent us back the way we came
and joked, in parting, "See you tomorrow!"

Perhaps we *would* see them —
it wouldn't be any more unlikely
than S. and me, strangers just last week,

sharing an orange on a beach
a mile from our room in Nafplio.
She takes the first bite, a rivulet

of juice dribbling down her chin
as she mashes the pearly cells
to pulp. I kiss her chin clean,

thinking all the while of the statue
that caught my eye on a visit
to Athens's Archaeological Museum.

A seeming burn victim, sculpted
as much by chisel as by sea,
the marble sloughing off like skin,

the statue appeared at first glance
to depict the death of Hercules,
as he tore at the blood-soaked shirt

and came away with steaming rags
of flesh. In this case, though,
barnacles had affixed themselves,

not fabric, petrifying over time
and therefore becoming synonymous
with stone, mussels on muscles.

Two millenia—that's how long
the statue waited to be found,
lost in a shipwreck off Antikythera,

forgotten by all but sea creatures
and to them just another rock
to settle down on, no more special

for having been made by hand
and with, I don't think it a stretch
to assume, no small amount of love.

Love—Eliot's "unfamiliar name
behind the hands that wove
the intolerable shirt of flame"

not even Hercules had power
to remove, not without removing
pieces of himself in the process—

isn't what binds S. and me together,
though I can foresee a future
in which I'll come to believe it was,

imagining what could have been
had I canceled my flight home
and stayed on with her in Greece.

Not love, no, nor convenience—
we're bound by the knowledge
that what we have won't last long,

take comfort in the inevitable
parting. At last, taking a bite,
I'm surprised how tart the orange is,

how much it burns my throat
going down, its juice a liquid fire
that leaves my lips frozen in a pucker.

The Death of Argos

1.

A few key seconds haven't yet come back,
if they ever were recorded. Who can say
why the dogs didn't, finally, attack,

much less what would've happened if they did?
On foot, defenseless, we were easy prey
to start with—then my cousin and I slid

into a ditch, scrambling to get away.
The footage skips ahead when I replay

this moment, picking back up with his leg
already broken and the dogs at bay—
or nowhere to be seen, at least. Less vague

is what came afterward: the brief but none-
too-gentle ambulance ride, the X-ray
revealing that the break was a clean one.

2.

The incident put me in mind of S.,
whom I'd been trying not to think about
for a few months, not wanting to address

how cruel I'd been when I abruptly stopped
texting and calling her back; stopped without
so much as an excuse, letting her opt

both of us out. Of course, our falling out
wasn't what I reflected on en route

to the hospital. Rather, it was her own
encounter with a dog, which left no doubt
a deeper scar than the two running down

her chin, down from the edges of her smile.
She told me that she didn't run or shout;
was, when the pit bull lunged, still in denial.

3.

Still in shock, sleep all but impossible,
I read the journal from my trip to Greece
after returning from the hospital;

read long into the night, about the night
when, meeting for a drink, we found release
from loneliness; about how S., despite

knowing me all of an hour, felt at ease
enough to share how many surgeries

she'd had to have in the last year, her face
still not quite hers; about the binding lease
that forced her to recover in the place

next door to where the pit bull went on living;
about its owner, who refused her pleas
to see the dog put down; about surviving.

4.

May 28th — Watching from the top deck
as Paros shrinks on the horizon, then,
in an instant, vanishes; as each new speck

becomes an island, looms, recedes from view.
On my way back to Athens, once again
on my own, though we plan to rendezvous,

S. and I, just as soon as she gets in.
It's strange how quickly things can happen when

abroad, that we could meet and fall in love
(is there a faster-acting medicine?)
on the same day; that I, at this remove,

perhaps because of it, could know we had.
Stranger still, that the scarring on her chin
should be what drew me to her, though I'm glad

5.

it did. We met on a bus taking her
to Naousa (rhymes with "wowza"), where I'd been
the day before, and taking me, as per

my host's advice, to drafty Golden Beach.
We chatted till she disembarked, within
those few short minutes managing to reach

the same conclusion. With this very pen,
on a scrap of paper torn from this Moleskin,

she jotted down her number. Pausing here,
I flipped to the back pocket, where the ten
digits had lived for almost half a year;

though I had no intention, not that night,
of calling her, no clue how I'd begin
to explain myself. "I'm sorry" sounded trite.

6.

Memories of the trip came flooding back:
I rendezvoused with S. in Nafplio
after the ferry ride, first losing track

of time, then of myself, as I explored
her body with my own, getting to know
each corner more each night, what she adored

and didn't, taking things both fast and slow.
I learned, as well, where she was born (Bordeaux)

and worked (at a high school in Athens), that
she taught biology and had done so
in Cairo during the youth coup d'état—

but not her age. I never learned her age,
which was, since she had both an olive glow
and graying hair, impossible to gauge.

7.

June 3rd—This morning I was moved to tears
by a brief passage in the Odyssey,
in which Odysseus, some twenty years

after he sailed for Troy, comes home to find
his old dog Argos cast out like debris
on a dunghill, by freeloaders inclined

to think this king disguised as nobody
had died an early death somewhere at sea.

I read it on the bus to Corinth, S.
asleep on my left shoulder, probably
for one of the last times, as we have less

than two whole days together, till my flight
departs from Athens and this fantasy
concludes—as I don't think we'll reunite.

8.

"Did Argos see the true Odysseus
or recognize beneath his beggar's clothes
the man he used to be, was previous

to leaving Ithaca?" I asked myself
while flipping through the epic, as the rose-
red light of dawn enveloped the bookshelf.

My hope was that the passage would disclose—
I don't know what. An answer, I suppose.

What fell out, rather, was a Polaroid
I'd put there for safe keeping, one of those
I'd taken while in Greece, of a deep void

near Corinth, a canal that ran as far
as S. and I—while standing on our toes—
could see, which even then recalled a scar.

9.

Early that morning, I got on the road
to see my cousin, straining to recall,
while driving, that lost moment, to decode

a scrambled memory (if there was one)
of our assailants and the sudden fall
that fractured time before it broke his bone.

Again, I saw two shadows—that was all—
come crashing through the nonexistent wall

around their yard, the wall we hoped was there,
and then keep running, with intent to maul
or kill or both, giving us such a scare

that we could do little but retreat—retreat
into a ditch as deep as we were tall
and, on a dark night, painfully discreet.

10.

Those few key seconds never did come back,
not on the drive there, nor in the time since—
time that I've wasted trying to unpack

that night, believing (wanting to believe
yet in the end unable to convince
myself) that if I simply could retrieve

the missing footage, I'd find evidence
that no such thing as a coincidence

existed, that there was a reason why
I'd had my own near-death experience
just three months after learning, by and by,

how S. had come to have her scars, and thus
that we were meant to meet, that providence
had shone its light on, of all people, us.

EPILOGUE

One memory that has come back, and does
so often, is of the stray dogs we met
at that canal near Corinth, where, because

we'd missed our bus and had some time to kill,
we took turns photographing the sunset
dissolving in the water like a pill.

It was at the station, though, when we were set
to leave, that the odd couple — a briquette-

black mastiff and his wiry, pint-sized friend —
entered the picture. Both affectionate
and filthy, they proceeded to offend

most everyone there, all except for S.,
who seemed, for one brief moment, to forget
her scars, letting each dog give her a kiss.

In-Flight Entertainment

The screens fold down only after we've
begun to descend, blinking to life
with footage of our plane—live footage,
it would seem. A glance out the window

to my left confirms this impression,
the mountains in one duplicated
in the other, a runway in both
taking shape. When the landing gear

folds down, it occurs to me how odd
it would be were something to go wrong;
were one of our jet engines to, say,
inhale a few unlucky seagulls,

flames and bloody feathers spewing out
the other end, all of it captured
on camera and played back for us
in real time, in what would have to be

the most exciting, not to say fun,
documentary we'd ever watch,
we who would be dead in mere seconds,
who till the last would hope against hope

for a Hollywood ending. Of course,
in all likelihood the plane won't crash,
just as I probably won't contract
my mother's cancer. It's more likely

that I'll change lanes into a semi
or have an aneurism before
my seventy-first birthday party
(if that age isn't wishful thinking),

that something I've never even thought
to fear will get me. The same is true
of everyone on board, yet our eyes
remain glued to the screens, just in case.

Then the footage suddenly freezes,
pausing on a short strip of runway—
an image blurred into abstraction
by the speed at which we're descending.

In Transit

ENTER AT YOUR OWN RISK—the signs were posted
at every entrance to the cemetery,
advising not to loiter under branches
or climb on toppled monuments. A windstorm
had swept through months before. In the time since
little had changed, the graveyard still a war zone
of craters where root systems used to be,
of headstones turned to rubble, pine to timber.
We wandered through the wreckage, reading names
that once filled address books, graced envelopes
and uniforms, erupted from the stands.
Family names that had been handed down
through generations, losing here and there
a letter, but surviving. Our own names,
Claire and Nick, which we made a game of finding,
wrapped up as we were in ourselves. "How sad,"
we said, about one boy's too-early passing.
The words *RETURNED WITH HONOR* were inscribed
below two dates, just fourteen years apart,
and a school portrait, probably his last,
embedded in the marble, capturing
Derek Ray Dunford at that awkward age
one lives, if one is lucky, to regret.
Claire told me what we needed was perspective
when, a mere four weeks later, she decided
to take a break—decided for us both.
It's why I'm writing this now, calling up
images from that walk, of the bowed limbs
barely supporting the half-leveled trunk

of an enormous ponderosa pine,
of how we stood, unthinking, under that
live weight, the branches buried deep enough
to serve as roots for the uprooted tree,
pillars on which it could, for a time, depend.
The cemetery lies between her place
and, at the bottom of the hill, my own.
I visit often, hoping we'll cross paths,
conversing with her in my mind, discussions
that always end with me convincing her
why we should be together, though I realize,
at the same time, it shouldn't take convincing.
On my last visit, seated on a headstone
designed to be a bench, what should I see
but a coyote, its antenna-ears
aware of but not bothered by my presence,
its black eyes closed against the wintry sunlight
descending through the foliage of two
still-standing cypresses. The trees converged
over two graves, no doubt a married couple's,
forming an archway meant to signify
that love, at least their love, is everlasting.

III

Palimpsest

Hold your eye level with the dining table
To see how much its reclaimed pine remembers
The scars of thirty years   of dropped utensils
Bumped glasses   long-forgotten meals
And arguments   of homework going back
To junior high   the layers of equations
Running together as if part of one
Long problem worked out over your whole childhood
Mixed in with your late mother's to-do lists
Her notes reminding you to feed the dog
Clean up your room   help out your older brother
With chemo dates   her doctor's number   checks
Made out to hospice and the mortuary
The verses you considered for her headstone
And the black eyes of pried-out nails   suggestions
Of a past life in England   one of many
Boards taken out of an abandoned barn
The wood not young but still impressionable

Valediction at Lake Livingston

My brother takes a crowbar to the dock,
prying it apart board by board. As if
exhaustion were the purpose of this trip,
he works all day. Our relatives unwind
on our stepfather's boat, a scar-white wake
lingering after they speed off. Inside,

our mother sleeps, retreating deep inside
herself, her body ravaged, like the dock,
by efforts to repair it. Loath to wake
because it forces her to wonder if
only and why and when, to tend these wounds
inflicted by her now impending trip,

she sleeps all day. Another kind of trip,
The Tempest beckons from my lap. Inside
its pages is a world where even wind
can be controlled—controlled but not, as doc-
tors say, prevented. Stopping only if
asked to, wearing a distant, half-awake

expression that my brother—now awake
to his past faults—ascribes to ego trips
and youth, I read all day. Jealousy if
not pride (according to the voice inside
my head) keeps me from helping with the dock,
the feeling palpable as a headwind.

As I approach Act V, my thoughts rewind
one month: faced with more chemo in the wake
of surgery, our mother used the dock's
rebuild as an excuse for this lake trip.
Clearly distressed, she must have known inside
what we now know but still deny, as if

accepting it would make her worse, as if
we had a say. Sunburned, filthy, and winded,
a Caliban through and through, both inside
and out, my brother trudges off to wake
our mother, helping her through the whole trip,
each step of the way down to the new dock—

which will resemble the old dock inside
a decade, if I had to guess. One trip,
the wind will pick up, and we'll hold its wake.

Nocturne

The nights I stayed at MD Anderson,
tossing and turning on that green recliner
or wandering the halls, went on and on.

Post-op, bedridden in a johnny gown
and socks, my mother put on fresh eyeliner
the nights I stayed. At MD Anderson,

her nurses knew me as the quiet son
who studied poetry (with a psych minor)
and wandered the halls. They went on and on

about my mother's strength, fooling no one
when they described her pain meds as "designer."
The nights I stayed at MD Anderson,

I made excuses to be on my own,
forgetting her room number (eight or nine or . . .)
to wander the halls, on and on and on,

sometimes till morning, waiting for the sun
to whisk me away like an ocean liner.
The nights I stayed at MD Anderson,
wandering its halls, would go on and on.

Rats

Night embellishes the sound that wakes me, disguises
　　its provenance. Before my eyes
adjust, I can see my stepfather in the kitchen
　　performing his "secret" ritual,
rooting through the fridge to prepare three or four
　　generous snacks out of assorted
leftovers. Once, I caught him dismembering a
　　rotisserie chicken the neighbors
had brought over, swallowing the cold, rubbery poultry
　　as he had their condolences
earlier that day.
　　　　　　　Getting up
　　for reasons beyond me, a puppet
struggling to find the overhead's dangling string,
　　I reach out and jam my finger
on . . . a bookcase? Suddenly wide awake, the pain
　　shooting up my arm, changing
my perception of the space, I maneuver past
　　poets who fell with gymnastic
grace from the bumped shelf, knowing where I am and what
　　to really blame for the unsubtle
rustling that woke me. My kitchen, however,
　　is empty—*my* kitchen, a heaven
for what seems an ever-expanding family of rats.

　　In the darkness pulses an atom
of light: the device that emits a high-pitched noise
　　more effective than poison
at getting rid of pests (according to its packaging).

I kneel down and, as if back
in time, am once more listening to the baby monitor
    my stepfather took it upon
himself to install, desperate to relieve us from
    the both painless and numbing
job of watching my mother rest; am once more embarrassed
    to be helping my own parent
change out a colostomy bag, to be depriving
    of basic dignity so very private
a woman. After the funeral, my stepfather unearthed
    a box of old photos that further
exposed her reticence. She'd kept us in the dark
    about everything from embarking
on a career in the army to running away from home
    at fifteen. It was as if someone
else had raised me and married him, not the woman depicted
    in those nicotine-yellow pictures,
whom we'd never get to know.
                              Standing up,
    I notice scraps from my supper
strewn across the kitchen floor, a literal trail of breadcrumbs
    leading to where rats shredded
the plastic wrapper of a half-eaten loaf. Even
    without my glasses, I can see
the worm of one's tail sticking out from a framed photo
    from our last vacation, as though
part of it, as though growing out of me, the son
    smiling while the Gulf thunders
at his back, his arm around his mother, who smiles, too,
    in the face of an uncertain future.

Gutting the House

Gulls kettle in the steam
    rising from what,
from meters up, must seem
    like tea bags but

for the smell; seem themselves
    sign of the Third
Coming, as their gyre delves,
    bird after bird,

into the dump. We've come
    to offload more
swamp-green linoleum
    scraped from the floor

of my brother's new house
    (new in a sense,
for there were previous
    owners, whose chintz

curtains and taste in flooring
    suggest a life
both eccentric and boring).
    My brother's wife

stayed behind to begin
    priming the walls
of dining room and den,
    her overalls

flecked as if with bird poop . . .
     Silly, that word.
It threw me for a loop
     when I first heard

a doctor opt for it—
     instead of "stool,"
"feces," or even "shit"—
     and keep his cool

explaining why our mother
     would yet again
need chemo, how another
     tumor had been

detected in "her pipes,"
     and what her odds
now were. She'd come to grips,
     she said, with God's

plan, was dead within weeks.
     Into the blue
compactor, whose breath reeks
     and teeth can chew

metal like bubblegum,
     we throw the last
strips of linoleum,
     then turn back. Past

turfed-over hills of trash—
　　the tumuli
thriving under an ash-
　　gray, weathered sky—

extends a field of gulls,
　　hundreds or more
weighed down by bellyfuls
　　of apple core

and rot. The ones we shoo
　　refuse to budge,
simmering as we stew
　　and all but nudge

them off the gravel drive.
　　We wonder how
they manage to survive
　　on foods that grow

a downy coat as thick
　　and white as theirs,
when our mother got sicker
　　despite our prayers

and an all-natural diet
　　of mostly kale.
("Don't knock it till you try it!")
　　Her death's gone stale,

having been talked to death,
    yet it's hung over
this weekend like the wreath
    we can't quite ever

bring ourselves to take down,
    the one that sheds
on her plot those crisp, brown
    tears. Sheds and sheds.

Housesitting

for William Logan

Meant only to evict, the chemical
kills dozens in the process. In between
furious calls to pest control, I screen
the porch: beneath the corner pedestal,
their former home and new memorial,
the bees start piling up—a hill of bean-
sized corpses mounting to, then past, obscene . . .
Out of the country, on sabbatical,

my host requests an update every day,
worried about his non-invasive guest
equally, it would seem. My rent-free stay
comes to an end in three months, which invests
it with the sweetness of a honey jar's
last drops. And yet, like the remaining bees,
which carry on as if their calendars
went on forever, sowing tapestries
of flowers as they pollinate the garden;
or like my mother in her final weeks,
a captive of her body, not its warden,
fed like a child while wasting through physiques
unfit for someone twice her age—I stick
to a routine. Habits are hard to kick,

but finding substitutes is harder yet . . .
Listening to old voicemails on the porch
tonight, soothed by her voice, though counterfeit,
I mistake a rising hum for static; lurch
forward then. Undulating like a net,
the whole hive sweeps across the yard, in search.

Explaining Myself

Form, my teacher averred,
can protect against outpourings
of emotion such as occur
after a loss, advice I followed
when documenting the toll
cancer caught late took on you,
subjecting peers in workshop
to accounts raw as they were
rigid (a villanelle whose two
repeating lines suggested remission
and relapse; a double sonnet,
an Elizabethan enclosed within
an Italian's octave and sestet,
about bees that took up residence
in a porch hollow of a house
where I was myself a guest,
the metaphor growing labored
when I tied infestation to disease;
a sestina sodden with perspiration
and sibling rivalry the more
insidious for going unacknowledged,
which relocated *The Tempest*
to South Texas, land of storms
capable of toppling a boat dock,
as one proved the summer,
your last, your first born sought
to find out if sweat can expel
grief, pouring himself into work;
a long-imagined, never-finished

pantoum on the bed-swing,
most southern of southern comforts,
my brother's rendering of which
weighed as much as four men
could carry, a hulking mass,
coffin-dense, its construction rushed
to ensure it saw you through
your last days, you whom chemo
had winnowed to a matchstick,
who, swaddled for warmth,
suspended as in water, rocking
back and forth, slept like a baby),
subjecting myself to critique
and, worse, infinitely worse,
to pity—
        form, that bulwark.